Fruits

BY ALLISON LASSIEUR

A⁺

Smart Apple Media

© 2015 Smart Apple Media, an imprint of Black Rabbit Books
P.O. Box 3263, Mankato, MN 56002
www.blackrabbitbooks.com

Cataloging-in-Publication Data is available from
the Library of Congress
ISBN: 978-162588-285-1

Published by arrangement with Amicus.

Editors: Rebecca Glaser and Tram Bui
Series Designer: Kathleen Petelinsek
Book Designer: Heather Dreisbach
Photo Researcher: Kurtis Kinneman

Photo Credits: Shutterstock/Darren Baker, cover; Superstock/
Chris Cheadle/All Canada Photos, 5; Shutterstock/Vorobyeva,
6; Superstock/Corbis, 9; Superstock/imagebroker.net,
10; Shutterstock/Roxana Bashyrova, 13; Alamy/Edwin
Remsberg, 15; Shutterstock/gopause, 17; Shutterstock/Anan
Kaewkhammul, 18; Shutterstock/romvo, 21; Shutterstock/
Crepesoles, 22; Shutterstock/jakit17, 25; Shutterstock/Elena
Itsenko, 26; Shutterstock/Monkey Business Images, 29

Printed in the United States of America at Corporate Graphics
in North Mankato, Minnesota.

10 9 8 7 6 5 4 3 2 1

Table of Contents

What Are Fruits?

What is a fruit? Fruit is the part of a plant that protects the seeds from harm. Fruits taste good. People eat them. Animals eat them, too. The seeds drop on the ground. Soon, they grow into new plants.

Berries are popular fruits
in many countries.

Each fruit has a different type of seeds.

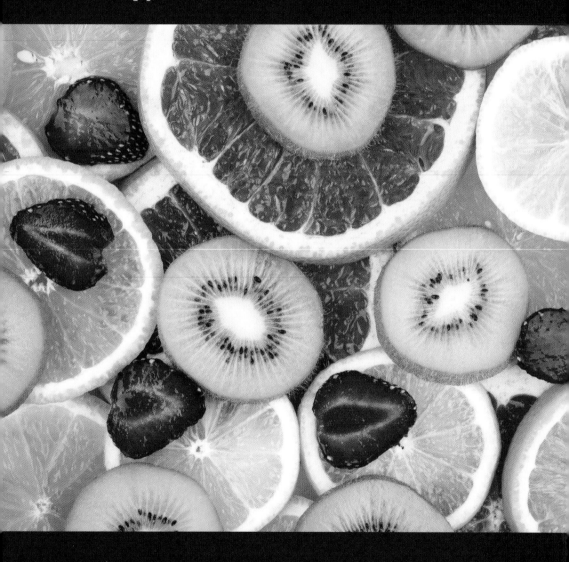

Q What types of fruits are there?

What is the difference between fruits and vegetables? Fruits cover the seeds of a plant. Some vegetables cover seeds, too. Most fruits are sweet and juicy. Most vegetables are not sweet. Another difference is that vegetables can come from other parts of the plant. They might be leaves, stems, or roots.

 You can choose from melons, berries, tree fruits, and **citrus** fruits!

Have you ever heard "An apple a day keeps the doctor away?" Fresh fruits have lots of **vitamins**. They have more vitamins than other foods. Eating fruits can keep your body healthy. Fruits can also help prevent many illnesses. You won't get super powers from eating fruits. But you will get a strong body.

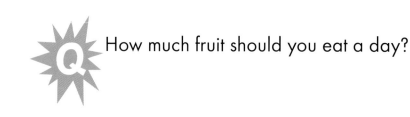 How much fruit should you eat a day?

An apple is a healthy, tasty snack.

 Kids should eat 1 ½ cups (375 mL) of fruit every day. One whole apple, banana, or orange counts as 1 cup (250 mL).

Cherry trees flower in spring.
The cherries grow in summer.

Where Do Fruits Grow?

Fruits grow in many places. A garden of fruit trees is called an **orchard**. Apples, pears, cherries, and peaches grow on trees. Blackberries and raspberries grow on bushes. Grapes and strawberries grow on vines. Fruit plants need a lot of sun. The dirt should not be too wet. It can't be too dry, either.

Each state has its own fruit crops. Georgia is known for juicy peaches. New York grows crisp apples. Maine **harvests**, or gathers, crops of wild blueberries. But many fruits come from just eight states! California, Oregon, Washington, Texas, Michigan, Pennsylvania, New York, and Florida grow more fruits than any other states.

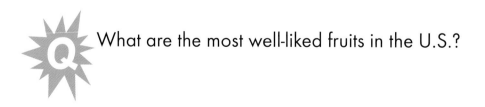 What are the most well-liked fruits in the U.S.?

Many peaches grow on trees in Georgia.

A Bananas top the list! The others are apples, oranges, grapes, and strawberries.

Traveling Fruits

Americans like to eat fruits all year. But fruits only grow during certain times in the U.S. It is summer in South America when it is winter here. Farmers in South America grow summer fruits. Then they send them to the U.S. That is how we can enjoy summer fruits like strawberries in the winter.

These crates of fruit are being shipped from Chile.

Many people like bananas. But they aren't grown in the U.S. or Canada. Bananas, and many fruits, grow in other countries. They grow in **tropical**, or very hot and wet places, such as South America. The U.S. and Canada **import**, or bring in, fruit for us to eat.

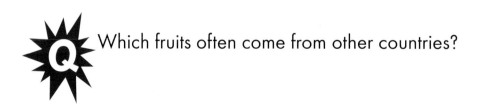 Which fruits often come from other countries?

Banana trees grow in hot, wet climates.

 A Mangoes come from India. Limes, grapes, and tangerines come from nearby Mexico.

Some fruits travel thousands of miles to your table. A banana is one of them. Bananas grow in bunches on trees. A worker cuts them down. The green bananas are loaded onto ships. The fruit will turn yellow on the trip. Trucks take the bananas to grocery stores. There, you can buy a fresh banana and enjoy it!

Bananas grow on trees in bunches of about 200.

Fruits Around the World

Have you heard of a small, fuzzy fruit with green pulp on the inside? It's a kiwi! The kiwi is native to China. It is also grown in New Zealand.

Fruits in your grocery store come from many countries. One reason is that people move to the U.S. from other countries. They miss fruits they ate back home. Another reason is that people like to try new foods.

Kiwi was first grown in Asia, but now it is enjoyed around the world.

Have you ever heard of a rambutan? It's from Asia. It's called the "hairy fruit." Another Asian fruit is the durian. It smells like rotten onions. But inside it is sweet and creamy. The dragon fruit is from Mexico. It's bright pink with crunchy black seeds.

The dragon fruit has a mild taste, like a cross between a kiwi and a pear.

Jackfruit is the biggest tree fruit in the world. One jackfruit can weigh up to 80 pounds (36 kg)! How do you eat a fruit that big? It's not easy. First you have to cut through the hard outside. Inside you'll find sweet, chewy fruit. People also like to eat the crunchy jackfruit seeds.

Jackfruit can grow larger than watermelon.

Eat lots of different fruits to get all the vitamins you need.

Healthy Fruits

Everyone knows that fruits are good for you. But why is this true? Fruits are loaded with vitamins. They also have **antioxidants**. Antioxidants protect the body from illnesses. Citrus fruits, such as oranges and grapefruits, have vitamin C. Vitamin C helps heal cuts. It also keeps your teeth and gums healthy.

How much fruit should you eat? Half your plate should be filled with fruits and vegetables. It's not hard to add fruit to your meals. Toss some slices of banana on your cereal. Drink fruit juice instead of soda. Snack on berries and yogurt. Add dried fruits to a salad. Mix different fruits to make your own fruit salad!

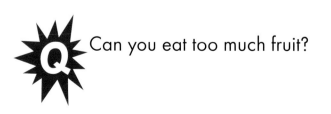 Can you eat too much fruit?

Berries are a tasty topping for waffles.

 Sometimes. Fruits are healthy, but they also have sugar. Be sure to eat a balanced diet that includes all the food groups—not just fruit!

Glossary

antioxidant A substance that keeps the body healthy.

citrus A juicy fruit that grows on a tree and has a thick rind, such as an orange.

harvest The gathering of crops that are ripe.

import To bring into a place or country from elsewhere.

orchard A garden or farm of fruit trees.

tropical To do with the hot and rainy places in the tropics.

vitamin One of the substances in food that is necessary for good health.

Read More

Aboff, Marcie. *The Fantastic Fruit Group*. Mankato, Minn.: Capstone Press, 2012.

Borgert-Spaniol, Megan. *Fruit Group*. Minneapolis: Bellwether Media, 2012.

Kesselring, Susan. *Eat a Rainbow: Healthy Foods*. Minneapolis: Magic Wagon, 2012.

Websites

Choose My Plate
www.choosemyplate.gov/

Eating Well with Canada's Food Guide
www.hc-sc.gc.ca/fn-an/food-guide-aliment/index-eng.php

Fruit and Veggie Color Champions
www.foodchamps.org/

Nourish Interactive
www.nourishinteractive.com/kids

Index

About the Author

Allison Lassieur tries to eat plenty of fresh, good foods at every meal. She has written more than 100 books for kids. Allison especially likes to write about history, food, and science. She lives in a house in the woods with her husband, daughter, three dogs, two cats, and a blue fish named Marmalade.